About the Book

Over two thousand years ago, a band of courageous Jews, led by Judah the Maccabee, vanquished the Syrian conquerors of Israel. Their story, found in the Apocrypha of the Bible, is one of the great epics of the western world. It is also the story behind the Jewish festival of Hanukkah.

This festival commemorates the rededication of the Temple in Jerusalem by the Jews after their victory over the Syrians.

In a style filled with Biblical overtones, Betty Morrow retells the heroic tale for modern boys and girls. Storytellers and librarians will find here at last a rhythmical version of the Hanukkah story that can be told or read aloud.

The latter parts of the book sketch in the historical background and explain the meaning of Hanukkah.

A Great Miracle is a story that will be of interest to all boys and girls who enjoy reading about heroic deeds.

A GREAT
MIRACLE

A GREAT MIRACLE

THE STORY OF HANUKKAH

by BETTY MORROW

Illustrated by HOWARD SIMON

 HARVEY HOUSE, INC.
Publishers
Irvington-on-Hudson, N.Y. 10533

To
David
and
Daniel

ONCE long ago, in the village of Modin in the land of
Israel, there lived a pious man with five strong sons. His name
was Mattathias. He and his sons farmed their plot of land,
followed the time-honored customs of the Jewish people,
and enjoyed the simple life of village folk.

These were dark days in Israel. The heavy tramp of foreign soldiers was heard in the land. The sword of the conqueror was stained with blood, and fear stalked abroad.

Then up rose Mattathias in terrible anger, and his sons with him, to fight the battle of the people. They left their home and their land and went up into the barren wastes of the mountains. There they lived with the open sky for a roof and a stone for a pillow.

Judah, the third son of Mattathias, was a shining youth. He was strong as an oak and proud as a young eagle. And the fate of Israel rested in his hands. It happened in this manner:

The land of Israel, the home of the Jews, was a tiny country lying at the crossroads of the ancient world. Many invaders had swept across it—Babylonians, Egyptians, Greeks —and some had ruled in the holy city of Jerusalem, but the Jews bowed their heads to none of them. They worshiped God, observed the Sabbath, and kept the laws of their people handed down from the time of Moses.

In the days of Mattathias, Israel was ruled by a Syrian king, Antiochus by name. He was a cruel and ambitious man who dreamed of conquering a mighty empire that would stretch from Persia to Egypt. He raised a great army, laid heavy taxes on the people, made war on his neighbors, and tried to win every man, woman, and child in his realm to his own purposes. But, save for the wealthiest among them, the Jews wanted nothing to do with Antiochus and his wars.

In Modin, Mattathias spoke out boldly against the king's schemes. "Remember the acts of our fathers," he said to his sons, "and be zealous for God and our laws."

At last Antiochus decided to have done with these troublesome Jews once and for all. Knowing that their religion was the dearest treasure in life to them, he issued a decree forbidding them to practice it. Everyone in his kingdom must

worship the Greek god Zeus. The penalty for disobedience was death. As a vile insult to the Jews, Antiochus looted the Temple in Jerusalem, burned the holy books, and set up a statue of Zeus on the altar. He stole the rich treasures of the Temple and took away the sacred lamp—the great golden menorah with its seven branches.

Antiochus sent soldiers through Israel to force the Jews to worship Zeus, but hundreds held their heads high and refused. They were slaughtered without mercy.

When this terrible news came to Modin, Mattathias cried out, "Woe is me! Why was I born to see this misery of my people and our holy city of Jerusalem?"

One day the soldiers came to Modin and set up an altar to Zeus in the marketplace. Mattathias and his five sons strode into the village square. Their neighbors huddled together to watch them.

"You are an honorable man in Modin," the captain of the soldiers said to Mattathias. "Now come first and listen to the king's command and bow before Zeus."

"Never," thundered Mattathias, "though all others in the king's realm turn away from their gods and obey him!" And Mattathias and his sons stood tall and proud before the soldiers.

"The king will honor you with silver and gold and many gifts," said the captain.

But Mattathias only answered, "We will not listen to the king's words or depart from our religion to the right hand or to the left."

Then a frightened Jew walked up to the altar and began to make a sacrifice to Zeus. In a rage Mattathias seized a knife, struck the man down, and knocked over the altar.

18

Turning to the crowd, he shouted, "All who are zealous for the law and the covenant follow me!"

Mattathias and his sons fled to the hills. Many Jews came to join them in the fight against Antiochus. The oppressed and the insulted made their way secretly into the mountains. Farmers left their fields, craftsmen left their shops in the towns. Whole families sought refuge with Mattathias in the wilderness.

Antiochus sent soldiers to destroy the rebels. But the Jews knew every rock and cave in the hills, and more often than not the soldiers returned empty-handed.

One evening some Syrian soldiers came upon a band of Jews—men, women, and children—who were hiding in a cave. The Syrians made their camp before the mouth of the cave, certain of victory on the morrow.

In the morning the soldiers called to the Jews in the cave, "Come forth, and you shall live."

But the Jews would not answer, nor would they lift a hand to defend themselves. For this day was the Sabbath which they kept as a holy time of rest and worship.

The soldiers threw burning brands into the cave and killed them all.

When Mattathias and his sons heard of this, they grieved for their dead comrades. Then Mattathias declared,

"Whenever the enemy comes to do battle with us on the Sabbath, we will fight. Nor will we all die like our brothers who were murdered."

Mattathias was an old man. When he felt death close upon him, he called his five sons to him and said, "Be valiant,

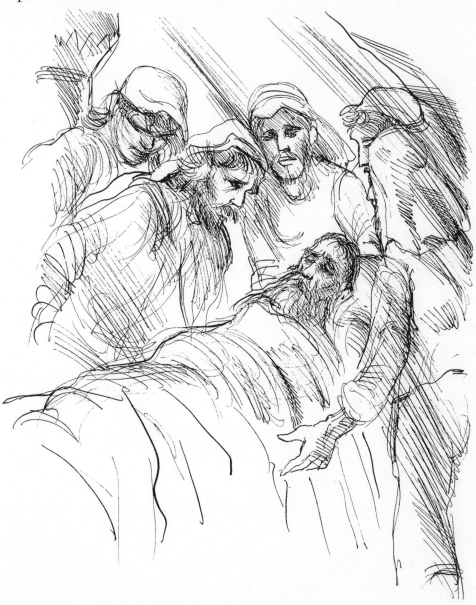

my sons, on behalf of the law, and avenge the wrong of Israel. Judah, your brother, has been mighty and strong from his youth up. Let him be your captain and fight the battle of the people.''

Thus Mattathias died, and Judah was chosen leader in his place. He was bold and skillful in war and could lead his men against the hosts of the enemy, like David the King and the heroes of old. Men called him Judah the Maccabee, ''Judah the Hammer of the Lord.''

Now a certain Syrian general, Appolonius, took an army into Israel, thinking to win glory, wealth, and the king's favor. When Judah saw the Syrians approaching, he strapped on his great breastplate. Fierce as a lion, he came down out of the wilderness, with his men following him.

In the heat of battle, he sought out Appolonius and killed him with a mighty stroke of his strong young arm. When the Syrians saw their general fall, they turned and ran. Judah took Appolonius' sword and fought with it all the rest of his days.

Antiochus sent a great army to rout Judah and his followers out of the mountains. The Syrians marched down

the plain of Sharon to the hill of Beth-horon. Ragged and
hungry, Judah's men were afraid when they saw such a great
number coming against them.

"How can we—few as we are—fight such a host?" they asked.

But Judah was unafraid. "We are fighting for our lives and our laws," he answered simply.

Judah and his men swooped down from Beth-horon. The Syrians did not know the narrow paths through the hills. The Jews darted at them from behind every rock. In their heavy armor the soldiers were slow and clumsy. Harassed on every side, the Syrians fled. Judah and his men seized arms, food, and the rich booty that the soldiers had left behind.

News of the Syrians' defeat traveled swiftly from one end of Israel to the other. By twos and by fives and by tens, Jews came to the wilderness, until Judah's band of hundreds grew into an army of thousands.

Antiochus gathered soldiers from all over his realm and sent an even greater army into Israel. As they marched, the sun gleamed upon a sea of helmets which filled the plain. The Syrians were so sure of triumph that merchants followed the army, believing there would be many Jewish prisoners to sell as slaves.

The Syrians planned to surprise the Jews and to take them in the dead of night. But Judah sent spies into the Syrian camp and learned of their plan.

At dusk he called his men before him. Danger hung over them like a thundercloud. All was as quiet as the last moment before a storm.

Judah spoke gently at first. "Any among you who are newly married," he said, "or who have planted young vines, or those who are afraid, go now before the battle, as is our custom." When no one departed, his voice rose in a war cry. "Arm yourselves and be brave, for it is better to die in battle than to look upon the misery of our people."

He divided his followers into small bands, each with its captain. Then he and his men left their camp with the fires still burning, and hid in the secret places of the wilderness.

In the middle of the night the Syrians stole into Judah's camp. It was empty. They searched for Judah vainly in the darkness, getting lost and finding nothing. At dawn they straggled back to their own camp. There, through the smoke of their burning tents, they saw Judah and his men waiting for them. In terror they ran for their lives.

For three long years the Jews harried the tyrant Antiochus. The king sent one army after another to take Judah the Maccabee, but the Syrians were defeated again and again.

Then Judah said, "Our enemies are vanquished. Let us restore the land of our people and our holy Temple."

One winter day in the Jewish month of Kislev, Judah the Maccabee and the Jews who had fought with him for so long, marched once again into Jerusalem. They found the Temple filthy and defiled. The great doors were charred by fire. Weeds grew in the courtyard. The altars were broken, and pagan statues stood in their place.

Judah ordered the Jews to cleanse the Temple and to dedicate it once more to God. The gold and silver treasures were gone, so they fashioned a new altar and a new menorah.

When it came time to light this holy lamp, only one tiny cruse of sacred oil could be found—just enough to burn for a single night. And eight days were needed to prepare new pure oil.

The priests poured the few drops of oil from the cruse into the menorah. Striking two flints together, they lighted it. Surely it would flicker out during the night! But the next day all seven branches of the menorah were aflame—and the next—and the next.

Anxiously they watched the lamp as it burned brightly against the winter darkness. By a miracle the oil lasted for eight days!

On the eighth day Judah and his people held a great celebration. Like a river of light they wound through the streets of Jerusalem to the Temple where the menorah burned.

"O give thanks unto the Lord," they sang, "for He is good, and His mercy endureth for ever."

The tyrant Antiochus was defeated, the Temple was cleansed, and the Jews could worship God and live by their own laws.

So for the first time they celebrated Hanukkah, the Festival of Lights.

Judah and the people of Israel declared that each year from that time forth the Jews should keep this holiday with joy and gladness. And so it has been to this day.

"*Nes gadol hayah sham*," say the Hebrew words. "A great miracle happened there."

And what was the great miracle? Was it the tiny cruse of oil that burned for eight days? Or was it the triumph of a band of brave men who staked their lives against the mighty hosts of the tyrant?

What Came After

All this happened over two thousand years ago. The time of rejoicing was short. For the war was not yet ended, even though the Jews had regained their holy city. Although Antiochus died the following year, the Syrians kept on sending armies into Israel.

In one battle Eleazar, Judah's younger brother, gave his life for his comrades. The Syrians brought terrifying, heavily armored war elephants against the Jews. Eleazar killed the lead elephant, but he himself was crushed by its great body when it fell.

When peace came again, Judah felt safe enough to marry and to live like other men. But this happy time was soon over. Once again the footsteps of Syrian hosts sounded in Israel. Judah was forced into hiding when the Syrian general, Nicanor, hunted for him even within the Temple.

Once more Judah and his men waited for the Syrians at the pass of Beth-horon, and again they put the enemy to flight. Among the dead was Nicanor himself. Judah proclaimed the Feast of Nicanor in honor of the Jews' victory.

The people of Israel returned to their homes, hoping to lead quiet lives, but this peace lasted less than a year. The Syrians came again with thousands of well-armed soldiers on foot and on horseback. The Jews had been quarreling among themselves, so Judah had only two thousand men at his command. He took to the hills as he had done before. He planned a surprise attack, but this time the Syrians were ready for him. When the Jews saw the great army drawn up against them, many of them fled in panic. Judah tried in vain to rally them.

The Syrians crushed the Jews between the two halves of their army. Judah and his few men fought desperately, but the hopeless battle was lost.

Judah the Maccabee was killed. Sadly his brothers took his body and buried it in Modin. All Israel mourned their dead leader.

Then Jonathan, the youngest son of Mattathias, brought fresh hope and courage to his defeated countrymen.

Like Judah, he, too, went through the land with a small band of men, darting at the Syrians from the hills and the marshes. John, the eldest of the five brothers, joined Jonathan in this outlaw life, and died in battle.

For seventeen years the Syrians advanced and retreated by turns. Jonathan built a string of forts, and slowly but surely drove the Syrians closer and closer to the borders of Israel.

Jonathan was a clever leader. He knew how to win allies as well as battles. Seeing that Israel was too weak to stand alone against the Syrians, he sent messengers to Rome. He even made friends with the boy king of the Syrians and so gained a few short years of peace for his people.

Again the peace came to a violent end. Tryphon, an ambitious general who was plotting to overthrow the young king, lured Jonathan into his hands with promises of friendship. A prisoner and a hostage, Jonathan watched helplessly as yet another Syrian army marched through Israel.

A third time the Syrians were stopped at Beth-horon. They retreated, taking Jonathan with them. He was put to death alone in a strange land.

Simon, the last of the five brothers, now stepped forward to give new heart to the despairing Jews.

"Your brother Simon is a man of wisdom," old Mattathias had once said to his sons. "Listen to him always."

With Simon at their head, the Jews drove the invaders out of their land. Simon became king and ruled in peace for the rest of his life. The Jews could live and worship as they wished without fear.

Israel was free.

Hanukkah, the Festival of Lights

The story of Judah the Maccabee and his brothers is a true one, a page in the long history of Israel.

No one knows who first told the legend of the tiny cruse of oil that burned for eight days. In the beginning it must have passed from one person to another by word of mouth. Hundreds of years later, when the Jews had been driven from Israel, the miracle of the cruse of oil was written down among the teachings of the wise men. To people living far from their native land, this legend of the Hanukkah lights surely brought hope and courage.

Just as Judah the Maccabee ordered so long ago, the Jews still celebrate Hanukkah for eight days with joy and gladness.

Every year in the middle of December, each family brings out a small menorah, a candlestick with eight branches, in memory of the lights that burned for eight days in the Temple in Jerusalem. In the evening the candles are lighted in a special manner—one on the first night, two on the second, and so on, until all eight candles are burning merrily on the last evening. The menorah also holds a ninth candle—the *shammash,* or servant—which is used to light the others.

As they light the candles, the family says a blessing: "Praised be Thou, O Lord our God, Ruler of the World, Who didst wondrous things for our fathers in days of old at this season."

Sometimes the family sings Hanukkah songs. Some are solemn, like the hymn *Maoz Tzur,* "Rock of Ages." Others are short and gay, like "Dreidl, dreidl, dreidl, I made it out of clay." A beautiful old folk song, "O Hanukkah," tells about a family celebration where the children are playing with their dreidls, or tops:

"And while we are playing,
The candles are burning low.
One for each night,
They shed a sweet light,
To remind us of days long ago."*

During the eight days of Hanukkah, a special menorah with eight lights burns in the synagogue each evening, while a prayer of thanks is recited. In Israel great outdoor menorahs light up the winter night.

Hanukkah is not one of the High Holy Days, the important feast days of the Jewish year; yet this festival has its own beauty and meaning. The candles speak of a history filled with heroic men and women who gave their lives for the right to worship God and to follow their own laws in a world full of cruelty and hate. To all people, the Hanukkah candles say that freedom is bought by struggle, that brave men are ready to fight for their beliefs.

*From Eisenstein, Judith. *The Gateway to Jewish Song.* New York, Behrman, 1939 (reprinted 1948). It is also included in Boni, Margaret Bradford, ed. *Fireside Book of Folk Songs.* New York, Simon and Schuster, 1947.

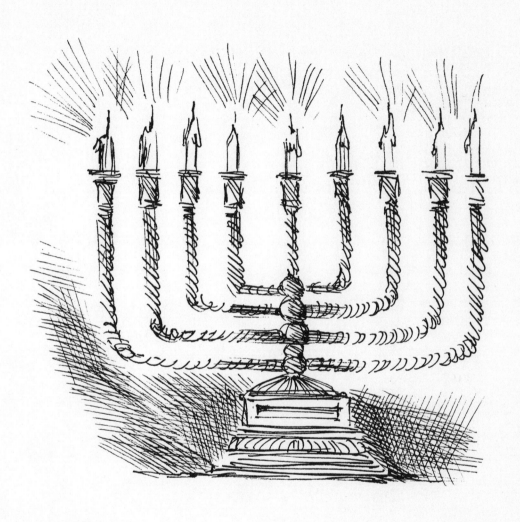

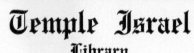

About the Author

at the University of California provide excitement enough for anybody!

About the Artist

BETTY MORROW is a children's librarian. She wrote *A Great Miracle* because she felt the need of a tellable version of the story of Hanukkah. This is her fourth book.

After graduating from Bryn Mawr College near Philadelphia, she lived in New York for many years and finally migrated to California about fifteen years ago.

She is the mother of two boys in their late teens, and now lives in Berkeley, California, where, she says, the students

HOWARD SIMON, painter and book illustrator, homesteaded in the Ozark Mountains, lived for many years in France and in the Far West. Today he lives in upper New York State. His subject matter derives mainly from historic source material as well as from the natural world that surrounds him. Besides illustrating adult literary classics, his work includes many books for younger readers.

Howard Simon is also represented by prints and paintings in many public and private collections.